Never Give Up!

Jiannetti expected to go in the first ten rounds of the 2000 Major League Baseball amateur draft. That never occurred. The Mets eventually picked him in the fortieth round.

Jiannetti knows why teams were gun-shy on draft day. "It was the diabetes that scared them away," he said. "After the Colorado Rockies found out about my condition, they backed off and the other teams lost interest, too."

ൠ ൠ

While Mormando drove home from Manhattan one rainy night, just a few days after the exhibition, a reckless driver slammed into his vehicle and almost ended his life.

Mormando remained conscience throughout the entire ordeal. As the paramedics strapped him to a backboard, all he could think about was getting back to martial arts.

ൠ ൠ

Born with motor oil in her blood, Sutton dreamt of the day when she would follow in the tire tracks of her grandfather, Ed, and father, Charlie, both popular race car drivers in their days.

Just as Sutton's dream began to blossom, exhaustion and episodes of numbness on the right side of her body caused her to miss several competitions, jeopardizing her promising racing future.

Running Through Roadblocks

Inspirational
Stories of
Twenty Courageous
Athletic Warriors

Jerry Del Priore

Bedazzled Ink Publishing Company * Fairfield, California

© 2008 Jerry Del Priore

All rights reserved. No part of this publication may be reproduced or transmitted in any means, electronic or mechanical, without permission in writing from the publisher.

978-1-934452-03-5 paperback

First published 2008
cover art and design by C. A. Casey

Interior photo credits
J. Peterson, Joe Zanolle
S. Fisher, Louis Verne
K. Sutton, courtesy of Kelly Sutton
M. McMaster, courtesy of Molly McMaster
R. Snow, courtesy of Randy Snow
J. Billauer and J. Del Priore, Jerry Del Priore
C. Galan, Jerry Del Priore
M. Utley, courtesy of Mike Utley
J. Jiannetti, Veronica Valentine
M. Bryant, courtesy of Mary Bryant
P. Mormando, courtesy of Paul Mormando
K. Romain, Jerry Del Priore

Cover photo credits
J. Peterson, Joe Zanolle
S. Fisher, Louis Verne
J. Jiannetti, William Hauser
M. McMaster, courtesy of Molly McMaster
P. Mormando, courtesy of Paul Mormando
M. Bryant, courtesy of Mary Bryant

Fletching Books
a division of
Bedazzled Ink Publishing Company
Fairfield, California
http://www.bedazzledink.com/fletchingbooks

Running Through Roadblocks *is dedicated to two special people who are no longer with us today: My Cousin Jerry Imbriano and my long-time neighbor and maternal figure Maryann Donadio.*

The author wishes to acknowledge that great efforts have been made to ensure that this book be as up to date as possible at press time.

Disclaimer

The medical information in *Running Through Roadblocks* is brief and strictly informational.

The author disclaims any liability for the decisions made based on the medical information in the book. It is not intended to replace the advice or expertise of a doctor.

Please consultant a license physician if you have any questions regarding the medical information in *Running Through Roadblocks*.

Acknowledgments

First and foremost, I would like to thank the twenty phenomenal athletes who allowed me to tell their amazing stories.

Secondly, I am grateful to the following special friends and colleagues for their support and guidance: Philip S. Blake and Jeanmarie Tari; Billy Casalaspro; Paul Todaro; Debbie Lyons; Paula Lizzi; Jill Adler; Jackie Robinson of Stavros Entertainment and everyone at Bedazzled Ink Publishing.

Thank you to the photographers who supplied me with awesome pictures, and my buddy Steve Giordano, who scanned several of their photos.

Many heartfelt thanks go out to my loving parents, Vito and Phyllis Del Priore; and my Aunt Marie Leone and Cousin Tina Leone. Thank you also to my sister Louisa; her husband Sal; and their beautiful children, Marisa and Carmine who I love as my own.

In conclusion, I will never forget the encouragement that all the special people in my life gave me during the research and writing of *Running Through Roadblocks*.

God Bless!

Table of Contents

Introduction	13
Jeff Peterson	15
Jim Eisenreich	21
Joe Jiannetti	26
Paul Mormando	31
Karl Romain	36
Brian Ruhe	40
Shaun Fisher	43
Jim Kyte	47
Molly McMaster	51
Photo Montage	56
Mike Utley	58
Randy Snow	61
Jennifer Andres	64
Cheryl Sheckells	67
Jesse Billauer	71
Andy Parr	75
Cody Colchado Jr.	78
Christine Galan	81
Mary Bryant	84
Kelly Sutton	89
Paul Martin	92
Afterword	97
Foundations and Businesses	98
Sports Terms Glossary	100
About the Author	101

Introduction

On the playing field, athletes are depicted as modern day gladiators. They run at incredible speeds, jump to heavens, and move the immovable objects. In a nutshell, they do things most sports fans wish they could do.

Do athletes deserve the superhero status that society has bestowed upon them? Well, it depends who you ask. To me, it's more than just pure athletic skill that makes an athlete special. The most commendable ones know how to conduct themselves on and off the field. They also go the extra mile to be positive role models to children.

At twelve years old, my doctor diagnosed me with Type I diabetes (juvenile diabetes), which occurs when the body doesn't produce enough insulin—the hormone that helps metabolize glucose (sugar)—or ceases manufacturing it all together.

Diabetes forced me to make drastic changes to my lifestyle. I stopped eating sweets, started measuring my blood glucose levels a few times a day, and injected myself with insulin twice daily: One shot before breakfast and one before dinner.

Everything happened so quickly. It scared and confused me. Thankfully, the doctors eased my burden by encouraging me to continue to exercise and play sports. The world of athletics brought my life enormous pleasure. I played and watched just about any sport.

During my ten-day hospital stay, I insisted on having

a television in my room so I wouldn't miss any baseball or football games. Sports helped me adjust to my new life as a diabetic. It helped cushion the blow.

As a child growing up in Brooklyn, I always cheered harder for the athletic underdogs. I felt inspired when I learned of an athlete who triumphed over adversity. It gave me the motivation to pursue my own dreams. I felt if they could do it, heck, so could I!

The athletes in *Running Through Roadblocks* share one common bond: They walked through the flames of adversity, but somehow emerged as champions after the ashes settled.

Employ their lessons in courage and fortitude to help you achieve the impossible, even when people are telling you it's improbable.

Jeff Peterson
An All-American Tribute

As a child, my Saturday mornings consisted of watching cartoons and my favorite past time, professional wrestling. Armed with powerful physiques and colorful personalities, pro grapplers were the closest things to real life superheroes.

When I first embarked on *Running Through Roadblocks*, I was hesitant to interview a professional wrestler. As much as I love the sport, I know there are some people that question its legitimacy.

One day while surfing the Internet, I came across an article on independent professional wrestler Jeff Peterson. After I read his inspirational story, I decided to contact him.

Our first interview took place at the ungodly hour of two a.m. When I picked up the phone, Peterson asked to speak to me while humorously disguising his voice. At first, his quirkiness caught me off guard. But as our conversation progressed, I began to develop a liking for this highly charismatic young man. His passion for life and wrestling impressed me.

Peterson's love affair with sports entertainment began at an early age. Perhaps being the nephew of Jim Kettner, owner and promoter of East Coast Wrestling Association (ECWA), had something to do with his deep admiration for the industry.

As a youngster, he was constantly backstage at his uncle's shows imitating the wrestlers' moves and over-the-top gimmicks. As Peterson grew older, he expressed a strong desire to learn how to wrestle.

At first, Kettner refused to enroll him in his wrestling school in Wilmington, Delaware, because of the high risk of injury associated with the training. After countless hours of persistent nagging by Peterson, he allowed his nephew to become a student at the grappling institution in order to keep him from trying to learn the sport in an unsupervised setting.

Peterson worked hard and took his instruction seriously. Although undersized for the sport, he truly believed that one day he would make it as a professional wrestler.

Not everyone shared his youthful optimism. His toughest critics said that his wiry physique had no business being in the ring. To his credit, Peterson ignored the naysayers and pursued pro wrestling with the bravado of a seven-foot giant.

"I am only five-foot-eight and one hundred and fifty pounds," Peterson said. "A lot of people told me I was too small to wrestle, but I never listened to them. I knew if I put in the time to learn how to wrestle properly, I would eventually get my chance to prove them wrong."

On March 21, 1998, at the tender age of sixteen, Peterson wrestled in his first match. Although he didn't win, he did show flashes of greatness, proving that he belonged in the squared-circle.

Sporting boyish good looks and a patriotic persona, Peterson earned the hearts of the fans and the nickname "The All-American."

But it was his superior technical skills and high-flying acrobatics that helped him develop into one of the top cruiserweights on the independent circuit.

Peterson captured two light-heavyweight titles in the South Florida area and participated in the 1999 and 2000 ECWA Super 8 tournaments—one of the most prestigious independent cruiserweight events in North America.

A rising star, Peterson couldn't help but feel optimistic about his future in the business. But on April 14, 2000, his doctor told him that he had developed lymphoma—a form of blood cancer.

Peterson was daunted by the doctor's news, but he refused to let it douse his star-spangled spirit.

"I was pretty bummed out when I was first diagnosed with cancer," he said. "But I knew I had to be strong to beat it. I was not going to let this disease get the best of me."

Peterson began chemotherapy soon after his diagnosis. He endured several painful sessions and even contracted pneumonia five times during the course of his treatments. But in June 2000, he went into remission.

Peterson talked about how pumped he was when he received word that he had beaten back the terrible illness.

"I kicked cancer's butt," he exclaimed. "I knew my belief in God and myself was going to get me through this."

Peterson decided to rekindle his wrestling career. But in order to reach his goal, he needed to get back into fighting shape.

Peterson's road back to the ring consisted of working out with a local high school wrestling team. He also instructed an energetic group of eight- to ten-year-old boys in various sports to help him stay active. The final step in his comeback occurred at a wrestling school in St. Petersburg, Florida, where he spent countless hours fine-tuning his grappling skills.

On April 6, 2002, Peterson stepped into the ring to wrestle in a match for the first time in over two years. With adrenaline coursing through his veins, he squared off against heel and veteran wrestler Ruffhouse Rivera.

The Delaware fans greeted the red, white and blue warrior with an enormous standing ovation. They roared with approval every time he executed a stunning move. Finally, after eighteen minutes of wrestling, he climbed to the top turnbuckle and nailed the supine Rivera with his signature Frog Splash move. Three seconds later, Peterson emerged victorious.

After the match, the crowd went wild for their beloved hero. Their overwhelming support completed his journey.

"It felt great to make my return to wrestling," Peterson recalled. "I put one hundred percent into my comeback and got one hundred percent back. I can't predict what will happen next in my life, but I will always be happy that I got the chance to wrestle at least one more time for the ECWA fans."

Unfortunately, Peterson didn't have much time to

celebrate his victory. On April 30, 2002, he returned to the Moffitt Cancer Center in Tampa, Florida, with a cancer relapse.

He asked his friend Annette to e-mail me the news and his hospital phone number. I developed a lump in my throat as I read the e-mail. I tried to choke back the tears but was unsuccessful.

That night, I called Peterson at the hospital to see how he was feeling. He didn't seem like the jokester I grew to love. Nevertheless, I knew he would fight the disease with every ounce of his being.

In July 2002 Peterson e-mailed to let me know that he went into remission. Sadly, the cancer returned just two months later, and on November 29, he passed away.

I read the news on a wrestling Web site. I stared at my computer screen for a few minutes before I broke down and cried. I was truly heartbroken over his passing. He was just twenty-one years old.

On November 30, 2002, IPW and NWA Florida Wrestling began their card by paying tribute to Peterson. Friend and fellow wrestler Naphtali informed the crowd that former IPW Light-Heavyweight Champion "The All-American" Jeff Peterson had passed away. He then asked the crowd for a moment of silence at which there was a ten-bell salute for their patriotic hero. After the tribute, Naphtali led the fans in chants of "Jeffrey . . . Jeffrey," as he draped an American flag across a turnbuckle. He went on to dedicate the show to the memory of Jeff Peterson.

Peterson and I wound up becoming good friends. We had chatted approximately ten times since our first interview, always talking deep into the night. I will never forget the courage he displayed during his battle with cancer. He taught me so much about life.

Though I never met him in person, we still connected on many levels. We shared a passion for baseball. I sent him several baseball cards to brighten his day. I know he really appreciated my gesture.

Jeff Peterson turned out to be more than an athlete I interviewed for *Running Through Roadblocks*, he became a cherished friend.

Although he has passed on, you can rest assure that one thing will always remain the same: Jeff Peterson is a true "All-American" hero in the eyes of many people, especially mine.

Jeff, I can still hear your joyous laugh. I love and miss you. God speed!

Jim Eisenreich

Hitting a big home run in a World Series game is what many children dream about. For former major league baseball player Jim Eisenreich, it not only happened once but twice in his illustrious career.

His first World Series home run, a three-run shot, came off of former pitcher Dave Stewart, leading the Philadelphia Phillies to a 6-4 victory over the Toronto Blue Jays in game two of the 1993 World Series.

Eisenreich's clutch home run helped bring his enigmatic condition—Tourette syndrome—a neurological disorder characterized by tics (involuntary, rapid, sudden movements or vocalizations that occur repeatedly in the same way)—out of the darkness and into the limelight.

"It felt great to help the Phillies win game two of the 1993 World Series," Eisenreich recalled. "Reporters asked me about my home run for two minutes, and then they grilled me about living with Tourette syndrome. I was okay with it. I was happy I was able to show people that a person with Tourette syndrome can succeed in front of baseball's biggest stage: The World Series."

But it wasn't always easy for Eisenreich, who began to exhibit symptoms (twitching, strange vocalizations and uncontrollable blinking) as early as six years old. No one knew why he displayed such strange behaviors. His family learned to live with it, but the outside world treated him as an oddity.

At school, the other children ridiculed and mimicked his mannerisms, and his teachers reprimanded him because they thought his behavior was an act of defiance. Eisenreich even had a junior high school football coach who mocked him when he repeatedly cleared his throat.

Eisenreich's doctor told his family that his bizarre actions were simply due to hyperactivity, and he would eventually grow out of it. As he grew older, his so-called hyperactivity (tics) didn't disappear.

To his credit, Eisenreich never let his symptoms prevent him from excelling in sports. In fact, his athletic ability was the only aspect of his life that his peers approved of.

"Growing up, sports, particularly baseball, helped me gain some acceptance from other kids despite my unique behavior," Eisenreich recollected. "When I finally started to play professional baseball, it was no longer accepted. My coaches and teammates didn't know how to deal with it, and neither did I."

On June 3, 1980, the Minnesota Twins selected Eisenreich in the 16th round of the 1980 MLB amateur draft. He spent two years in the minors annihilating opposing pitching.

In 1982 Eisenreich jumped from A-ball all the way to the Twins' roster. In his first thirty-four major league games, he hit an impressive .303 and played a stellar centerfield.

Unfortunately, his undiagnosed disorder kicked into high gear and made playing baseball a living nightmare.

On May 4, 1982, Eisenreich removed himself from a game against the Red Sox at Fenway Park when the bleacher fans' taunting caused his symptoms to flare-up beyond control.

Eisenreich sensed his baseball career slipping through his grasp. By June, the Twins placed him on the disabled list, ending his rookie season.

He received a variety of treatments including hypnosis and psychotherapy, but nothing seemed to help. Finally, a physician in Minneapolis diagnosed Eisenreich with Tourette syndrome. Even though he had an answer to his problematic behavior, his baseball career still encountered several pitfalls.

From 1983 to 1984, his condition limited him to only fourteen games. After the 1984 season, he decided to retire to concentrate on getting healthy. But Eisenreich knew in his heart that his love for baseball would bring him back to the game.

Just before the start of the 1987 season, with his medication properly adjusted, the Kansas City Royals claimed him off of waivers and signed him to a contract. After hitting a blistering .382 for Kansas City's Double-A affiliate in Memphis, Tennessee, the team called him up to "The Show."

From 1987 to 1988 Eisenreich batted .228 with five home runs and forty RBI in one hundred and twenty-six games. Even though he struggled, he persevered. In 1989 he rediscovered his sweet swing and stroked a solid .293 with 33 doubles and 27 stolen bases. His terrific campaign earned him the Royals' Player of the Year Award.

In 1993, Eisenreich signed with the Philadelphia Phillies and had one of his finest seasons in his career, batting an impressive .318 with 115 hits, seven home runs and 54 RBI.

The Phillies went on to capture the National League crown, and Eisenreich played in all six World Series games, driving in seven runs. In 1995, as an everyday player for Philadelphia, he hit .316 with 10 dingers and 55 RBI.

On December 3, 1996, Eisenreich signed a two-year contract with the Florida Marlins. In 1997, as a platoon player, he hit .280 and belted 20 doubles in 293 at-bats, helping the Marlins capture the Wild Card and the National League crown, respectively. His huge two-run homer in Game Three of the 1997 World Series helped Florida outslugged the Cleveland Indians, 14-11. The Marlins went on to win the 1997 World Series in a dramatic seven-game series.

"It was the most amazing feeling in the world," Eisenreich said of winning the 1997 World Series with the Florida Marlins. "The noise levels were overwhelming. Imagine 67,000 people going crazy. The celebration in the stadium went on for an hour and a half after the game ended."

On May 14, 1998, Florida traded Eisenreich, Gary Sheffield, Charles Johnson, and Bobby Bonilla to the Los Angles Dodgers for Mike Piazza and Todd Zeile. The following season, he decided to call it quits after he was unable to secure a spot with a major league team during spring training.

In 1996 Jim and Leann Eisenreich established The Jim

Eisenreich Foundation for Children with Tourette syndrome. The foundation helps children with TS achieve success through programs and services.

Eisenreich stated that only a small percentage of TS patients display coprolalia—the excessive and uncontrollable use of inappropriate language, something that the media has sensationalized.

Throughout his life, Eisenreich used his heroic spirit to help him overcome the numerous obstacles that almost prevented him from achieving a successful baseball career. He knows what it's like to face insurmountable odds, and uses his experiences to help children overcome adversity.

"I tell kids they can achieve anything they put their minds to," he said. "If I can make it, so can they."

If a Hall of Fame for courageous athletes existed, Eisenreich would make it in on the first ballot.

Joe Jiannetti

Nothing thrills me more than attending a live baseball game. The crack of the bat, a mammoth home run, and the aroma of warm peanuts and freshly mowed grass are some of the stimuli that awaken my senses.

I attended my first live baseball game at the age of nine. I was totally awestruck by the larger-than-life baseball atmosphere. Every time I see a little tyke at a game, all of those cherished memories come rushing back. It truly makes me feel like a kid again.

On June 25, 2001, the Brooklyn Cyclones, a minor league affiliate of the New York Mets, brought professional baseball back to the borough after a forty-four year absence.

It was an instant match made in heaven. Game after game, the hometown fans packed KeySpan Park and passionately rooted for their beloved team. The Cyclones electrified the Coney Island crowds with several come-from-behind wins during its inaugural season.

One day while thumbing through the newspaper, I came across an interesting article on Cyclone third baseman Joe Jiannetti. Just like me, Jiannetti is a juvenile diabetic.

At the age of fifteen, he began to experience the typical diabetic symptoms: Constant thirst, extreme fatigue and excessive urination. After Jiannetti lost eleven pounds in eight days, a teacher told him that he looked terrible and needed to see a doctor right away. Soon thereafter, his physician delivered the bad news.

"When I first found out I had diabetes I didn't know much about it," Jiannetti said. "I just knew I wouldn't be allowed to eat sugar."

Jiannetti's worries diminished as he learned more about the disease. He kept his condition in check by exercising, eliminating high carbohydrate foods, taking two daily injections of insulin, and measuring his blood sugar three to four times a day. He refused to let diabetes stop him from fulfilling his dream of playing professional baseball.

After Jiannetti graduated from high school, he waited for draft day to see which team would select him. Baseball scouts from the Minnesota Twins, Atlanta Braves, and Florida Marlins contacted him before the draft. He even had a productive tryout with the Pittsburgh Pirates.

Jiannetti expected to go in the first ten rounds of the 2000 Major League Baseball amateur draft. That never occurred. The Mets eventually picked him in the fortieth round.

Jiannetti knows why teams were gun-shy on draft day. "It was the diabetes that scared them away," he said. "After the Colorado Rockies found out about my condition, they backed off and the other teams lost interest, too."

Although the Mets drafted Jiannetti, they asked him to spend a year at junior college away from home to see how he would fare. He agreed, and enrolled in Daytona Beach Community College. In forty-five games with the Falcons, he hit a blistering .376 with eight home runs and six triples.

"They (NY Mets) wanted to see if I could take care of my diabetes when I was away from my family," Jiannetti said. "I took their advice and showed them I was able to manage my diabetes and play ball at the same time."

New York signed Jiannetti in June 2001 and shipped him to the Kingsport Mets of the Appalachian League (rookie league).

In late July 2001, the Mets promoted him to Brooklyn of the New York-Penn League (short-season A-ball) where he smacked an inside-the-park home run in his first game with the team.

Jiannetti went on to slug .348 with three home runs and twenty-nine RBI in forty-one contests, helping the Cyclones capture the 2001 NYPL Co-Championship*, the borough's first title since the Brooklyn Dodgers defeated the New York Yankees in the 1955 World Series.

Jiannetti spent the next three seasons playing the infield and outfield while moving up New York's minor league ladder. In 2004 he reached double-A ball with Binghamton, clubbing .353 with one long-ball and three RBI in five games.

His climb up the ranks was cut short the following year when the Mets released him after spring training due to the logjam of outfielders in their farm system.

Jiannetti wound up in the independent Can-Am League, splitting the 2005 season with the New Jersey Jackals and Grays (a traveling road team).

A few months before the 2006 season got under way, Jiannetti began using an insulin pump—a small mechanical device worn on the outside of the body that delivers rapid or short-acting insulin twenty-four hours a day through a catheter placed underneath the skin, enabling him to better manage his glucose levels.

With his diabetes in check, Jiannetti jumped to the competitive independent Atlantic League and enjoyed a career-year with the Atlantic City Surf, leading the club in average (.319), home runs (21), and RBI (79). His stellar numbers earned him a spot on the Atlantic League All-Star squad.

"It's so much easier to control your highs and lows with accurate insulin doses and not having to just guess like you do with a syringe," Jiannetti said of using the insulin pump. "It's hard enough to play baseball at a high level, but if you have diabetes and you can't control it, that makes it nearly impossible. The pump has made it realistic for me to play this game at a completive level."

Although the insulin pump helps him balance his blood glucose levels more efficiently, Jiannetti still has to eat periodically to avoid the drops associated with an active lifestyle, and always has food readily available when it occurs.

"Every day I pack a lunch box with two sandwiches—one for lunch and another for after batting practice along with some chips and maybe a cookie or two," he said. "I also have some candy in case my sugar level goes low. Then I make a peanut butter and jelly (sandwich) to take out to the field with me. I always got to have enough food (around). You never know."

After beginning the 2007 campaign in the Detroit Tigers' minor league spring training camp, Jiannetti returned to the Atlantic League (Newark Bears and York Revolution), where he set a league record with a twenty-eight game hitting streak dating back to his final twenty-five contests of '06 and his first three of '07.

Jiannetti continues to work hard and hopes to return to affiliated baseball in the near future. Moreover, he feels that as long as he adheres to a healthy lifestyle, his condition won't be a problem.

"As far as my diabetes goes, I know as long as I take care of myself, everything else will fall into place," the Florida native said. "I just want the chance to prove that I'm a good baseball player, and get a fair shot at the big time."

Jiannetti is determined to succeed in baseball despite diabetes. His positive attitude and hard-nosed style of play makes him a diamond in the rough on the diamond in the field, with plenty of luster left in his game.

Due to the tragic events of 9/11, the NYPL canceled the playoffs and declared the Brooklyn Cyclones and Williamsport Crosscutters Co-Champions.

Paul Mormando

As a small, timid child, Paul Mormando endured daily harassment and ridicule from the bullies in his Brooklyn neighborhood. It got to the point in which Mormando stopped going out to play because he feared further torment.

"Back then, I was a small, skinny kid. I was very shy," Mormando recalled. "It was very stressful when I couldn't go out to the park and play baseball because I was worried about who was going to take my bat and glove."

Driven by a desire to learn how to protect himself, a young Mormando begged his parents to let him join a karate school. At first, they rejected his request, but eventually allowed him to take lessons.

"My mother would be like, 'you're going to get hurt. Look how small you are.' She talked to my father and asked him to try and talk me out of it," Mormando said. "But finally, one day after nagging them, they gave in."

Mormando wasn't the most gifted kid in class, but made up for it with pure dedication to his craft. He spent an extraordinary amount of time practicing in his parents' basement in order to master the arts.

"I definitely wasn't the best in the class," he said, "but I was definitely the hardest working."

The countless hours of training turned Mormando into a martial arts machine. In fact, he became so well versed in the arts that he began to develop his own style called Cha Ki Do—a hybrid of fighting styles taken from boxing, wrestling, and other martial arts. As his art progressed, Mormando began to instruct his own students out of his parents' cellar.

Meanwhile, he continued to train at a Tae Kwon Do school run by "old school" Korean instructors. But when word got back to his senseis that he was teaching his own methods, they felt dishonored and disrespected and refused to let Mormando take his black belt test, eventually dismissing him from their school.

Upset and frustrated, Mormando decided to study other forms of martial arts in order to perfect Cha Ki Do. He earned his first two black belts in two different styles of Tae Kwon Do, then a black belt in Shotokan, one in Go Ju (Okinawan Karate), and the last in Jujitsu.

After several years of fine tuning Cha Ki Do, Mormando presented it to the World Professional Karate Organization (WPKO) for approval.

In 1990, the WPKO (headed by Grand Master Aaron Banks—an icon in the world of martial arts promotion) awarded Mormando a certificate to teach Cha Ki Do, making him one of the youngest, at the age of twenty, recognized Grand Masters in martial arts history.

Despite this honor, Mormando's tenth-degree black belt rank ignited a firestorm of controversy throughout the martial arts world.

"Most people didn't really believe that somebody my age could have that intellectual value to do that," Mormando said of developing his own style. "When I proved it to a board of martial artists, some were mesmerized and a number were very negative about it. It opened up for a lot of hardship, challenges, and battles."

Mormando ignored the naysayers and continued to teach Cha Ki Do to his pupils. When he could no longer accommodate his growing student body, he moved into his first school in Sheepshead Bay, Brooklyn.

After five years, he opened a second school and its collective membership increased to over five hundred students.

Mormando's martial arts legacy began to spread throughout New York City, prompting numerous requests for his services: He taught rookie NYPD officers his hand-to-hand combat techniques and educated NYC public school children on violence deterrence and self-discipline.

Soon thereafter, the entertainment field beckoned. Mormando appeared in a few episodes of NBC's *Law & Order* and had small roles in several action films. He even acted in the Off-Broadway (now Broadway) play *Tony and Tina's Wedding*.

While acting opened up a new world of possibilities for Mormando, he never lost his flair for displaying his dazzling martial arts skills. In July of 1993, he broke the board-breaking world record by shattering fifty-six boards in fifty-eight seconds before twenty thousand people at Shea Stadium and over two million TV viewers.

Mormando's amazing board-breaking demonstration helped elevate his martial arts career to a new level. The opportunities seemed endless. Unfortunately, his good luck came to abrupt end.

While Mormando drove home from Manhattan one rainy night, just a few days after the exhibition, a reckless driver slammed into his vehicle and almost ended his life.

Mormando remained conscience throughout the entire ordeal. As the paramedics strapped him to a backboard, all he could think about was getting back to martial arts.

His body had different ideas, though. Mormando couldn't move. Although not paralyzed, the accident had severely injured his neck and back, causing excruciating pain.

His doctor advised him to forget about martial arts and just concentrate on walking again. No more kicks or punches, just countless hours of traction and physical therapy.

No longer able to display the physical prowess that took him a lifetime to develop, Mormando slipped into a deep depression and was forced to shut down his schools and cease all martial arts activities.

"For a while, I was very discouraged," Mormando said. "I was down for months. I couldn't walk . . . I couldn't do anything. I was disgusted."

Fortunately for Mormando, he opted for acupuncture instead of back surgery, which began to heal him and started to lift his sagging spirits. But it was a muscular dystrophy telethon that helped put his life in perspective.

"I recall seeing some people who were a lot worse than I was," he said, "and it made me think that there were people that never have been able to witness their full physical potential because of that (disability).

"I think that was a very positive thing for me to see. It made me realize that maybe I wasn't that bad off."

Soon thereafter, Mormando began to stretch, and gradually rehabilitated his body in order to return to teaching.

It took five years, but in 1999—after losing the entire client base from his previous schools—Mormando opened a new school in Canarsie, Brooklyn. Today, over one hundred and forty students train at his dojo, and he continues to develop other martial arts side projects such as a documentary based on his life.

In addition to the aforementioned accolades, in 2003, the WPKO and Ring 8 (an organization comprised of boxers who assist former boxers in need) inducted him into their Hall of Fames at Madison Square Garden alongside fighting legends Bruce Lee, Chuck Norris, and Joe Lewis.

"I'm not a quitter," Mormando said. "That's definitely not in my mentality. If there's an obstacle in my way, I push it to the side and just keep going. The accident was just another obstacle."

Although time and injuries have taken away a portion of Mormando's martial arts abilities, his indomitable spirit soldiers on.

Karl Romain

Karl Romain boldly stated in his high school yearbook that he would capture a Kung Fu World Title before his twenty-third birthday. In April 1988, a serious automobile accident on the Tappanzee Bridge in Nyack, New York, threatened his world championship prediction.

Romain sustained severe injuries to his neck and back and spent eight long months in the confines of a cervical collar. His doctor advised him against a comeback, warning him that any type of trauma to his neck or back could result in paralysis. Despite the doctor's prognosis, Romain wasn't quite ready to give up his world championship pursuit. He refused to let the countless hours in the dojo go to waste, and wasn't going to let a roadblock prevent him from achieving his ultimate goal.

During his rehab stint, Romain attended several Kung Fu tournaments, which only reassured him that he could still defeat the top contenders in the sport, prompting this brave warrior to make a comeback despite the doctor's recommendation.

Asked why he was willing to take such a monumental

risk, Romain replied, "I didn't want to look back and regret not trying. I didn't want ten years to go by and think should've, would've, could've. I'd rather try and fail than have to regret not trying at all."

In the first two tournaments of his spirited return to competition, Romain took home two first place awards. In 1990, at the World Association of Karate Organization (WAKO) championships, he struck gold and became a World Champion at the age of twenty-two, fulfilling his prophecy and life-long dream, with the ever-present threat of paralysis looming.

"It's important to set goals," Romain said. "By making my goal public in my yearbook, I pushed myself every day to succeed."

Romain retired from competition in 1994 to focus on developing his marital arts school. In 1996, the International Kung Fu Hall of Fame inducted him into its prestigious institution.

While attending a martial arts tournament, the coach of the U.S. National Kung Fu team asked Romain if he was interesting in competing again. With a World Title and a Hall of Fame honor to his credit, he already had cemented his place in martial arts history.

Romain believed he still had the ability to take home more hardware and decided to accept the coach's invitation. In September 2000 Romain won silver and bronze medals in the Forms and Weapons Division at the Martial Arts World Championships in Kentucky. The following year, he took home the silver in the Forms Division at the World Championships in Vienna, Austria.

With all his competitive martial arts aspirations fulfilled,

Romain decided to permanently retire. "After winning my last silver medal, I felt that I had achieved everything I could," he said. "There was nothing else for me to prove as far as competition went."

After our interview, I had the pleasure of meeting a number of Romain's students and their parents. I quickly realized the positive impact martial arts training had on our youth. His students showed me a great deal of respect and their parents went on to tell me that Romain's guidance had played a vital role in helping their children grow as individuals.

"Martial Arts starts and ends with respect, and that is what I teach," Romain said. "Martial Arts is one of the most powerful vehicles for self-improvement, and I believe if everyone in the world understood the benefits of martial arts training, they would all do it. People of all ages would do it."

Romain's teaching skills are highly regarded in Nyack, New York and its surrounding areas. The New York Giants have retained his services to cross-train their football players during the off-season. A few of his star pupils include Giants star wide receiver Amani Toomer and former Giants tight end Howard Cross.

Toomer credits his improved focus, flexibility, and hand/eye coordination to the years of martial arts training with his instructor. "Sifu Romain has helped me become a better athlete," Toomer said. "He knows how to get the best out of people, and he does it in a positive manner."

Romain remains loyal to the art aspect of martial arts. He emphasizes this particular component to every student he teaches. "I'm not that into the sport element," he said. "A sport is a sport. The competition aspect is based on martial arts. It still has certain aspects that have the philosophy. The art itself isn't about competition; it's more about if you're going to compete, compete with yourself. How good can you be? Can you be the best that you can be?"

Since the inception of his first Martial Arts school in December of 1991, Romain has helped over ninety students earn their black sashes. Two of his students are members of The International Kung Fu Hall of Fame—a true testament to his teaching and leadership skills.

Having made such a tremendous comeback against the odds that faced him, Romain is a perfect example of what you can accomplish if you believe in yourself and are determined to reach your goals despite the challenges you encounter along the way.

Brian Ruhe

At the age of eighteen, Brian Ruhe was involved in tragic automobile accident, which took his girlfriend's life and resulted in a serious head injury and the amputation of both legs above the knee.

In an instant, his young life changed forever. At first, moving on seemed impossible to him, but as time passed by, he somehow found the courage to live again.

"My girlfriend's death got to me," Ruhe recalled. "I dealt with it, and now she's living through me."

Ruhe spent two and a half months in a hospital recovering from his injuries, followed by a year of demanding physical rehabilitation. Since his injuries were so severe, the doctors stacked the odds against a successful recovery.

An orthopedic surgeon told him it was pointless to try to use prosthetics to relearn how to walk, and a psychologist said he would never have the cognitive ability to finish college.

Ruhe remained optimistic despite the grim diagnoses.

"I knew the doctors were wrong about my prognosis," he said. "I knew if I stayed positive I could accomplish anything I wanted to. What they told me really motivated me to prove them wrong."

After rehabilitation, Ruhe played a variety of sports but nothing electrified him like ice sled (sledge) hockey—a version of the game played by athletes with various lower extremity impairments (e.g. amputations, cerebral palsy, and spinal cord injuries).

Each player sits on a sled two to four feet long with two hockey skate blades underneath the seat. They utilize two short hockey sticks with metal picks affixed on the ends to help handle the puck and dig into the ice to propel themselves about the rink.

"At first, I didn't know what sled hockey was, but I decided to give it a shot anyway," Ruhe said. "The first time I hit the ice, I immediately fell in love with the sport. It gives me a sense of freedom no other sport ever did. People are very surprised to see how cool this sport is. I know they're impressed by the action of ice sled hockey."

In January 2000 Ruhe began playing defense for the Rehabilitation Institute of Chicago Blackhawks. In August 2001, only a year and half after he took up the sport, he made the 2002 U.S. Paralympic sled hockey team.

Entering the Paralympics, Team USA held the sixth seed out of a field of six. No one expected them to win a medal. Fortunately for the red, white, and blue crew, they believed in themselves.

With inspired play, the U.S. squad mowed down squad after squad, making it all the way to the gold medal match against Norway. After a hard-fought forty-five minutes of hockey and a ten-minute overtime period, the teams wound up in a 3-3 tie. In the shootout round, the Americans lit the lamp three times, while the Norwegians only scored twice, giving Team USA a thrilling 4-3 victory and the top prize.

"I always believed we could win a medal, but I was pleasantly surprised when we took home the gold," Ruhe said. "It was an amazing feeling to see the red, white, and blue raised while the U.S. national anthem played. My eyes filled with tears of pride and joy for my country."

Ruhe enjoyed an incredible tournament, notching seven assists in six games, tying him for second place on the team in helpers. He also registered the third best plus/minus rating in the tournament.

Playing sled hockey only represents a portion of Ruhe's amazing comeback story. After his accident, he went on to earn his undergraduate degree in biomedical engineering from Wright State University. He is currently pursuing a Ph. D. in biomedical engineering at Northwestern University, where he hopes his research leads to the development and promotion of ultramodern prosthetic devices that will help amputees walk more normally one day.

The gold medal that Ruhe and his teammates won at the 2002 Paralympics represented more than a first place finish; it symbolized their indestructible fortitude, which helped them turn dark tragedy into gold triumph.

"When I was first injured, I never thought I could experience the joy I felt the day we won the gold medal," Ruhe said with jubilation in his voice. "We proved that anything is possible as long as you believe in yourself."

Shaun Fisher

Shaun Fisher had always dreamed of skating in the NHL. He played three years of junior hockey with the Plymouth Whalers of the Ontario Hockey League (OHL), establishing a reputation as an offensive-minded defenseman. In one hundred and seventy-seven regular season games with Plymouth, Fisher scored 133 points (29 goals, 104 assists), and added 32 more (5 goals, 27 assists) in forty-seven playoff contests.

On May 31, 2000, the NHL Carolina Hurricanes signed the undrafted free agent to a contract, bringing his dream one step closer to reality. Fisher was living large, but he would confront something more terrifying than a 6-2, 220-pound forward with a bloodthirsty mean streak.

In June 2000, while jogging at his home in Southgate, Michigan, Fisher began to gasp for air just ten to fifteen steps into his run. From there, his breathing got worse. He spent several sleepless nights enduring unbearable chest pains. His doctor eventually diagnosed him with asthma and prescribed medication accordingly.

After two weeks, Fisher still had trouble breathing. When

he began to experience excruciating calf pain, he checked himself into a hospital. The doctors discovered two blood clots: one is his leg, causing calf distress, and another in his lung, making breathing nearly impossible.

Fisher's blood clots were due to a rare hereditary blood disorder called congenital antithrombin III deficiency—a condition that forms clots in the arteries and/or veins, making blood flow difficult.

The doctors immediately put Fisher on blood thinners to dissolve the clots. Although the medication would save his life, any type of injury could cause him to bleed to death. The doctors told him to hang up his skates.

"I was devastated (by the news)," Fisher recalled. "Hockey was the only thing I pictured myself doing. It meant everything to me."

Refusing to give up hockey, Fisher made a phone call to the Hurricanes organization asking for their help. The Assistant General Manager of the Hurricanes referred him to Dr. Judith Andersen, a blood specialist from the Barbara Ann Karmanos Institute in Detroit, Michigan. What Dr. Andersen told Fisher changed his life forever. She knew of an injectable medication that would thin his blood, but not to the same extent as the pills, giving him a good chance at resuming his hockey career.

"It was a tremendous weight off my shoulders," he said. "I always felt something was out there to help me play again."

But before Fisher could start his new medication, which didn't guarantee him a shot at a professional hockey career, he had to wait six months for the initial blood thinners to leave his system. This meant he had to abstain from all forms of vigorous physical activity.

With six months to spare, Fisher enrolled himself in college, and did well, but he yearned for the frozen H2O.

In June 2001 Fisher began the injections, and within a month, he received the green light to lace up his skates and hit the ice again. The year he spent away from hockey helped him become more of a complete player and person.

"I now have a new outlook on life," Fisher said. "I have as much fun as I can have inside and outside the rink, and I don't take things for granted. Coming back from my illness has put my life in perspective."

Fisher attended the Hurricanes' 2001-02 training camp before he made his professional debut in October 2001 with the Florida Everblades of the ECHL (AA). In sixty-six games with Florida, he notched twenty-five points on four goals and twenty assists, with a plus/minus nine rating.

From 2002-2004, Fisher logged a few thousand miles while playing for five different ECHL teams: The Everblades, Greenville Grrrowl, Trenton Titans (twice), Texas Wildcatters, and Roanoke Express. Although he had frequently changed squads in that time span, he still managed to post decent numbers: 10 goals, 28 helpers, and 108 penalty minutes in one hundred and four games.

Fisher enjoyed stability and productivity during the 2004-05 season with the Kalamazoo Wings of the United Hockey League (UHL), where he registered 11 goals and 22 assists in sixty-five contests, helping Kalamazoo qualify for postseason action.

The five-foot-eleven blue liner returned to the ECHL for the 2005-06 season, playing with the Augusta Lynx, Phoenix Roadrunners, and Bakersfield Condors.

Fisher spent the next two seasons (2006-08) in the UHL,

now IHL, with the Flint Generals and Bloomington PrairieThunder, posting a combined 72 points (8g, 64a) and 156 PIM in one hundred and twenty-seven contests.

Fisher's solid play and unbreakable spirit makes him a solid hockey player with a good shot at moving up to the next level. But it's his positive outlook on life that helps remind us what really matters most.

"There's hope for everything out there if you really want it," he said. "You can come back from anything. If not, it could always be worse."

Jim Kyte

In his playing days, Jim Kyte personified the role of a hockey enforcer. As an imposing 6-foot-5, 220-pound defenseman, Kyte never had a problem with dropping his gloves and tangling with an opponent when the situation called for it. In 598 NHL games, he compiled an impressive 1,342 penalty minutes.

Although Kyte possessed a tremendous amount of physical toughness on the ice, his intestinal fortitude defined him as a player and also as a person.

Born with a hereditary hearing deficiency that caused degeneration of his audio nerve, Kyte began to gradually lose his hearing at the age of three. At five, he started using a large, awkward hearing aid device with long wires that inserted into his ears, which caused other children to taunt and tease him. But Kyte used hockey as his strength to ignore the ridicule from his peers.

Kyte spent two seasons in juniors with the Cornwall Royals of the Ontario Hockey League (OHL). Unfortunately, the harassment didn't stop there even at this level, as one of the opposing players used to call him "Radio Shack" because of his hearing aid.

That didn't prevent Kyte from having an impressive junior career, prompting the Winnipeg Jets to select him in the first round, 12th overall, in the 1982 NHL Entry Draft.

Kyte's hard work and steadfast determination helped him skip the minors and become the first legally deaf player to don an NHL uniform in 1982. He played a total of seventeen years of professional hockey, including thirteen in the NHL, where he skated for five different teams: The Jets, Pittsburgh Penguins, Calgary Flames, Ottawa Senators, and San Jose Sharks.

Because hearing aid technology proved so inadequate during his career, Kyte employed other methods to help him compensate for his hearing loss in professional playing situations. Since he had difficulty picking up sounds of hard-charging skaters bearing down on him, he relied on Plexiglas reflections instead to view the action around him. And while he chased down the puck in his own zone, he depended upon his goaltender for direction with arm cues to help him avoid the opposition.

As a child, hockey provided Kyte with the confidence to grow as an individual. As an adult, for eight years, he organized The Jim Kyte Hockey School for the Hearing Impaired in Ottawa, Canada, as a way to help hearing impaired and deaf children enjoy and learn the sport and improve their self-esteem in the process.

"I wanted to give hearing impaired kids a chance to play ice hockey," the Ottawa native said. "I know the positive influence hockey had on my life. I wanted those kids to experience the same incredible things I did."

As a young boy, Kyte always looked up to his dad, who

spent countless hours teaching him how to perfect his hockey skills. Today, many kids lack positive role models in their lives. So they sometimes look to athletes and celebrities for guidance.

Kyte, who has received several honors for his charitable work involving hearing impaired children, stated that he doesn't "agree with professional athletes who are unwilling to accept their responsibility as role models. Athletes should use their stature to put smiles on peoples' faces, especially the kids."

In 1997 Kyte had an off-season automobile accident. An ensuing concussion forced him to miss the entire 1997-98 season with post-concussion syndrome. He decided to retire in the summer of 1998.

"I was able to face my retirement with dignity," said Kyte, who still experiences the lingering effect of post-concussion syndrome. "It was easier to handle because I was told I wasn't medically fit to play as opposed to being told I was no longer good enough."

Ironically, Kyte suffered only one concussion in his entire professional hockey career.

Although the car accident ended his playing days, Kyte still managed to express gratitude for the opportunity to earn a living as a hockey player.

"Things happen for a reason," Kyte said of the injury that terminated his hockey career. "Not many people get the opportunity to play this great game and get paid for it. I'm thankful I had that chance."

Today, Kyte conducts public speaking events for schools and corporations, writes a weekly column for the Ottawa Citizen during the hockey season and coordinates the Sport

Business Management Graduate Certificate program at Ottawa's Algonquin College.

While Kyte misses the ice, being a father to his three boys (Hayden, Wyatt, and Owen) keeps him, as well as his wife, Nancy, very busy. Raising his children, though, takes precedence over anything else in his life.

"Someday, I would like to consider coaching hockey," he said. "But right now, my main priority is raising my three boys. They mean the world to Nancy and me."

Kyte epitomized the blue-collar type of hockey player: He worked hard, played physical, and always defended a teammate when the situation arose. But his ability to overcome his hearing impairment and skate in the NHL made him a fan-favorite wherever he played.

Molly McMaster

Molly McMaster will do just about anything to spread colorectal cancer awareness. But just how far will she go? Try inline skating from Glens Falls, New York, to Greenly, Colorado—a total of 2,000 miles.

An awful long way for one person to travel just to get a message across, but McMaster has her reasons.

In February 1999, after being misdiagnosed and enduring several months of unbearable pain, McMaster had emergency surgery to remove twenty-five inches of her large intestine (colon), along with a sizeable tumor.

McMaster spent the next few days in the hospital recovering from surgery. But on February 19, 1999, the same day as her twenty-third birthday, the surgeon told her that he had removed a malignant tumor and that she had Stage II colon cancer.

McMaster sat in her hospital bed incredulous at the diagnosis. Nothing her doctor said registered at the time.

"I remember nodding my head (in disbelief)," McMaster recalled. "My first reaction was, he's lying. I wanted to die. I couldn't go through chemo."

McMaster, known for her optimism and intestinal fortitude, threw in the towel and even had thoughts of suicide. She had a hard time accepting how a young, active female, who lived a healthy lifestyle and had no family history of the disease, developed colon cancer.

Later that morning, McMaster's friend Rocky called to wish her a happy birthday. She didn't want to tell him the bad news because she thought he might treat her differently. She finally pulled herself together and told him.

"That sucks, but you can beat it because you're Molly," he said, as a matter-of-fact reply.

Those simple but effective words helped her muster up the courage to fight back.

McMaster received eight months of IV chemotherapy. During that time, she searched for an answer to why her doctor in Colorado misdiagnosed her with constipation. She had all the symptoms but her doctor never once tested for colon cancer.

"I was so angry when I was first diagnosed because I was misdiagnosed the first time," McMaster said. "You can test for it and remove it before it starts."

Her doctor just inquired about her family's history of colon cancer. She never asked about colon polyps. If she had, she might have discovered that McMaster's mother had a polyp removed at the age of thirty-two. That factor alone made McMaster a high-risk for developing colon cancer and probably would have revealed the tumor sooner.

McMaster had symptoms in high school but didn't think much of them. She just didn't have enough information on colon cancer to know any better. Now, she has made it her business to inform people of the disease in the most unusual ways.

In addition to Rolling To Recovery—her 2000-mile Inline trek—McMaster has developed numerous other projects to educate the masses, including the Colossal Colon—a forty-foot long, four-foot tall, crawl-through model of a human colon.

McMaster wants to leave people, especially children, with an everlasting impression and wants them to know that anyone can develop colon cancer.

"My goal is for people's jaws to drop, and remember what I have done," the Wilton, New York native said. "I want people to look at me and think that I could never have had cancer. It doesn't matter what skin color you have or what language you speak, this is something that can happen to anyone."

McMaster began playing hockey in 1995 and quickly fell in love in with the game. She even played once a week while receiving chemotherapy. That type of drive and dedication helped her land a spot on the Adirondack women's ice hockey team.

In February 2000, her squad captured a gold medal at the Empire State Games, held in Lake Placid, New York, almost exactly one year after her diagnosis. In 2004, her team took home a silver medal, and then won a second gold in 2006.

In addition to serving as the president of the Colon Club, the nonprofit organization responsible for the Colossal Colon, McMaster held the community relations coordinator position for the now-defunct Adirondack Frostbite of the United Hockey League (UHL)—now the International Hockey League (IHL), a Double-A minor league.

The late Marc Potvin, former Frostbite head coach and

NHL player, came up with the idea of having her play a shift for the team to help fill the arena and promote colon cancer awareness.

They went to Richard Brosal, former president of the UHL, for approval. He suggested that she play a shift for all the teams in the association. In conjunction with the league, the Colon Club launched The UHL Cross-Checks Colon Cancer campaign.

On February 26, 2006, McMaster hit the ice for her first game, as Adirondack took on the Richmond RiverDogs at the Glens Falls Civic Center. During the month of March, which is National Colorectal Cancer Awareness Month, she skated in one home game for the additional thirteen UHL clubs to help promote the cause.

At first, McMaster thought some players might not support her endeavor because they would deem it as just a silly publicity stunt. To her surprise and delight, the players offered their support and encouragement.

"I was really nervous," McMaster said. "I didn't want to insult anyone. But the players in the UHL were all absolutely over-the-top welcoming. They went out of their way to make me feel like I belonged on their teams."

McMaster always wanted to try out for the U.S. Women's hockey team, but because of her illness, that never occurred. Her hockey quest more than filled that void. With a bigger event than anything she could have ever imagined, McMaster got the opportunity to reach an entirely new audience while playing the game she loves.

"Overall, this was by far, the most amazing experience I've ever had the opportunity to have, and better for me than playing in the Olympics any day of the week," the five-foot-eight blue liner said. "Not only can I say that I got to play men's professional hockey on fourteen different teams in the UHL, but I got to do the one thing that matters most of all: I got to show people that anyone can get colon cancer."

McMaster never imagined that her work would help so many people, but it has in a colossal way.

McMaster even encouraged one of her neighbors, who she first met at a Colon Club event in an Upstate New York mall, to have his colon examined. It turned out that he had three cancerous polyps, which the doctor quickly removed.

He approached her one day to let her know that her advice and knowledge saved his life.

"I never realized that so many people would be affected by my story," she said. "I feel I'm lucky to do this (cancer awareness) and help save lives."

It's the world that's lucky to have a crusader against cancer such as the unstoppable Molly McMaster.

Molly McMaster

Shaun Fisher

Jeff Peterson

Jesse Billauer & Jerry Del Priore

Kelly Sutton

Randy Snow

Running Through Roadblocks 57

Mike Utley

Karl Romain

Mary Bryant

Paul Mormando

Joe Jiannetti

Christine Galan

Mike Utley

On Sunday, November 17, 1991, in a football game at the Pontiac Silverdome, Detroit Lions' quarterback Eric Kramer called a simple pass play their offense ran all the time. Right guard Mike Utley dropped back into pass blocking mode to protect his quarterback. He then collided violently with a defensive player, lost his balance, and fell to the ground, ramming his head into the unforgiving turf.

Utley lay motionless on the field before several thousand stunned and frightened spectators. As medical personnel transported him off the gridiron, he flashed the crowd a "thumbs up," a getsure that would become a symbol of his heroic spirit.

Unfortunately, the result of the play fractured his sixth and seventh cervical vertebrae, paralyzing him from the chest down, ending a once promising football career.

The days that followed the accident tested him like nothing ever had. Although his future looked bleak, Utley faced his circumstances with tremendous courage and optimism.

On December 13, 1991, Utley began his rehabilitation program. The doctors told him that his days of walking were over, and if he didn't recover any sensation or movement in his lower extremities after the first six months to a year, his condition would never improve.

After a year, his lower body didn't respond, but Utley refused to give up on himself. He continued with his regimented rehab program, knowing in his heart that one day he would defy the odds.

Finally, after five years of relentless, grueling physical therapy, Utley regained slight movement in his toes. His modest progress encouraged him to step up his rehabilitation efforts even further.

His hard work paid off. On February 15, 1999, Utley took his first public steps (with assistance) since the accident.

"I just wanted to show people that the doctors were wrong about my prognosis," Utley said. "I pushed and pushed because I knew something was there."

Utley is classified as a "C-5-6-7 incomplete quadriplegic" (minimal sensation or motor control below the point of spinal cord lesion). Due to the fact that his injury is "incomplete" and he participates in an intense rehabilitation program, he has recovered various degrees of feeling and movement in his legs, hips, buttocks, lower back and extremities.

As remarkable as Utley's progress has been, his ultimate goal is to one day walk off the field where he suffered his career-ending injury.

"You got to push every single day," Utley said. "If you don't push every single day, you'll never get to where you want to be. You'll never get any further than where you are."

In addition to his vigorous workout regimen, Utley

participates in numerous highly challenging activities such as boating, kayaking, seadooing, water skiing, scuba diving, and hand cycling.

In December 1991, with the support of his agent Bruce Allen, he established the Mike Utley Foundation to raise funds to benefit research, rehabilitation, and educational programs for people with spinal cord injuries. Utley believes that a cure for paralysis is within reach.

"Clinical trials for a cure are not that far way," he said. "I continue to do my part in my rehabilitation program. Now, it's up to scientist to do their part so people like me can walk again."

When Utley is not rehabilitating his body or working with his foundation, he is publicly speaking throughout communities on reaching goals and overcoming obstacles.

Utley's resolve and philanthropic work have garnered him numerous prestigious accolades, including the 1997 Detroit Lions Spirit Award, which is now called The Mike Utley Spirit Award—an honor given to the player who best demonstrates excellence on and off the field.

In addition to the aforementioned honors, in February 2004, the Paralysis Project of America bestowed Utley with the Shoemaker Award, and Washington State University, his alma mater, inducted him into its Athletic Hall of Fame.

Although the injury has physically changed Utley, it hasn't altered the essence of his being one bit.

"No injury will ever change who you are unless you allow it to," Utley said with conviction in his voice.

Here's a thumbs way up to a great athlete and even better human being.

Randy Snow

At the age of sixteen, Randy Snow took a summer job working on a farm to earn some spending cash. Little did he know that his summer employment would drastically change the course of his life.

While operating a front-end loader, a 1000-lb bale of hay dislodged from its scoop and crashed down on Snow, nearly crushing the life out of his youthful body. He suffered four broken ribs, a punctured right lung, a compound fracture to his left arm, and a severely crushed spine, which paralyzed him from the waist down.

Snow spent the next few months in a rehab hospital, relearning basic living skills. After wallowing in denial for three years, he slowly began to accept his disability. But it was a return to sports that made him feel whole again.

"I was an athlete before I got hurt," the former junior tennis player said. "When I went back to playing sports, I went back to being who I was as an athlete and as a person."

To the general public, wheelchair sports are a commendable but diluted form of competition. For the athletes, it possesses a certain degree of cutthroat competitiveness that goes unnoticed by most sports fans. On numerous occasions, wheelchair athletes have exploited a "more disabled" competitor in order to win, according to Snow. It's a take no prisoners attitude that spells the difference between winning and losing.

The opportunity to participate in sports is immeasurable to the wheelchair athlete. Snow put it best when he said, "Wheelchair sports aren't for the people who need it; it's for the people who want it."

And no one wanted it more than Snow, who made a name for himself in the world of sports. He holds the distinction of being the only athlete to compete in three different summer Paralympics in three different sports, and win a medal in each sport to boot. Additionally, he belongs to an extraordinary group of elite athletes who have competed in both the Paralympics and Olympics.

At the 1984 Olympics in Los Angeles, California, as millions watched worldwide, Snow captured the silver medal for the U.S. in the men's 1500-meter exhibition wheelchair race. He also took home a gold medal as a member of the 1984 U.S. Paralympic Track Team.

In basketball, Snow represented the U.S. seven times in various wheelchair tournaments. In 1983 and 1986 he won gold medals with the U.S. at the Gold Cup World Championships. In 1996 he captured a bronze medal with Team U.S. at the Paralympic Games in Atlanta.

But it was tennis in which Snow made his mark, capturing ten U.S. Open singles and six doubles titles. At the 1992 Paralympics in Barcelona, Spain, he won two gold medals: One in singles competition and another in doubles. He is arguably the greatest wheelchair tennis player in sports history.

In 1996, the Atlanta Paralympic Organizing Committee asked Snow to receive the Olympic torch from President Bill Clinton at the White House to commence the Paralympic games.

"I will never forget the time I spent at the White House with President Clinton," the Texas native said. "It's something most Americans dream of doing."

Winning wasn't Snow's only objective when he battled it out on the playing field. He used sports to prove to the public that people in wheelchairs play an important role in society.

"Having a disability is just another human characteristic, like having a certain type of hair and eye color," he said. "Unfortunately, we are viewed as wheelchairs, rather than people using wheelchairs. Educating the able-bodied population is the key to changing this mentality."

On top of being a great athlete, Snow is also a published author and the president of NoXQS (no excuses) Inc.—a motivational achievement company.

Out of adversity came a champion athlete. Armed with a basketball, tennis racquet, and a sports wheelchair, Snow helped change the complexion of wheelchair sports. Not only did he dream big, he played bigger.

Jennifer Andres

For Jennifer Andres, playing professional football for the Baltimore Burn provided an excellent opportunity to showcase her overall athletic abilities. Although she had participated in numerous competitive sports, football tested her mental and physical fortitude like no other athletic pursuit ever had. Andres didn't mind. In fact, she met the challenge helmet-on and wound up falling in love with the action of the gridiron.

"It (football) was the most competitive sport I ever played," Andres said. "It brought out an aggressive side of me I didn't realize I had."

Andres always made it a priority to keep in tiptop shape. Sports and fitness played a huge role in her life. She even managed to stay physically active for eight full months while she carried her son Henry.

In the final month of Andres' pregnancy, she began to experience hot flashes. She thought it was due to her pregnancy, and it would pass after she gave birth.

In January 2000, her doctor delivered Henry. But after his birth, the hot flashes didn't disappear. To make matters worse, Andres developed several new symptoms: Depression, tachycardia (rapid heartbeat), extreme fatigue and an insatiable appetite.

Andres' doctor attributed her distress to postpartum syndrome and told her she would recover in due course. Unfortunately, as time passed, she didn't feel any better. No matter how much Andres slept, she still felt tired. She found it extremely difficult to enjoy her new bundle of joy.

"It was debilitating and frustrating and because all my symptoms were so vague, I felt like there was something wrong with me, but I wasn't quite getting the fact that I was sick," Andres said of the time her condition went undiagnosed. "I just felt so weak that it was scary."

Unable to obtain an appointment with four different internists, Andres luckily kept her regularly scheduled visit with her gynecologist. Her doctor decided to perform a full blood analysis to determine the cause of her distress. The blood tests revealed a condition called Graves' disease—a type of autoimmune disease in which the immune system over stimulates the thyroid gland, causing hyperthyroidism (an overactive thyroid).

A prolonged undiagnosed case of Graves' disease can lead to serious complications such as heart problems, birth defects in pregnancy, and in extreme cases, death. Presently, there is no cure for Graves' disease, but it can be managed with proper medication.

Andres' doctor prescribed two drugs to combat her overactive thyroid. Unfortunately, she was allergic to both. The next course of action included radiation therapy to control her overactive thyroid and artificial thyroid hormones to replace what the radiation wiped out.

The treatments were successful. Right before the 2001 NWFL (now the National Women's Football Association—NWFA) campaign began, her thyroid levels returned to normal. Andres went on to play the entire season, registering four sacks for the Burn defense.

"Because of Graves' disease, I have very little recollection of the first few months of Henry's life," she said. "I felt the disease took away six months of my own life. I don't know if I even can explain it, but it was absolutely one of the lowest points in my life. However, I am very thankful that I was healthy enough to play football."

Andres spent several years working as a high school guidance counselor, helping countless students prepare for brighter futures.

During her playing days, Andres embraced her responsibility as a positive role model to children. She never turned down a child's request for an autograph, and even spoke at a high school graduation as a member of the Burn.

"After the graduation, there were several boys who came up to me and asked for my autograph. It was real cute," Andres said, with a chuckle. "I think I got more respect instantly from those high school boys for what I did in football than I probably would have in a year of being their counselor."

Andres epitomizes today's American woman: A terrific athlete, a great wife and mother, a dedicated professional and a wonderful role model.

Although Graves' disease almost sacked Andres' spirit, she somehow found the courage to tackle adversity like a true winner.

Cheryl Sheckells

It takes a unique psychological temperament to play the defensive line in football. For instance, defensive linemen must be slightly demented, have an intense desire for contact and enjoy inflicting pain.

Former Baltimore Burn defensive "linewoman" Cheryl Sheckells personified the aforementioned traits. Her bulldozing style of defensive made opposing offenses shake in their cleats.

As physically menacing as Sheckells was on the gridiron, it was her mental toughness that made her a true sports heroine.

During her football days, she contended with several medical conditions, which made it very difficult for her to play. Sheckells somehow found the strength to suppress the pain and suit up for action.

Sheckells' medical problems started in her late twenties, when her right knee developed rheumatoid arthritis—a chronic inflammatory disease which causes the immune system to attack the linings of the joints, creating intense pain and swelling.

Since her diagnosis of rheumatoid arthritis, Sheckells

has undergone two operations on her right knee, with the likelihood of having total knee replacement surgery in the future.

Unfortunately, the condition has migrated to her hands, back, and ankles, causing further distress.

"Sometimes, it's a little tough to stand and walk," Sheckells said, "but I take medicine to help with the pain."

Unfortunately, her medical woes continued. After a few years of living with rheumatoid arthritis, Sheckells' doctor diagnosed her with bipolar disorder—a complex brain condition characterized by episodes of mania and major depression. An affected person's mood can swing from excessive highs (mania) to profound despondency (depression), usually with periods of normalcy in between.

Not only does Sheckells struggle to find the light through the darkness of bipolar disorder, she must also deal with the threat of unexpected panic attacks. Her day-to-day living is anything but easy, but she has several people in her life to help her cope with the illness.

"My meds can be thrown off by the simplest thing I do, so I have to monitor my life everyday," Sheckells said. "This illness not only affects me, but my family and friends also. They help me to monitor my life. They are my guardian angels."

Already burdened by two medical aliments, at the age of thirty-five, Sheckells developed congestive heart failure—a condition in which the heart is unable to pump enough blood throughout the body to meet its physical demands.

Sheckells is well aware of the stress CHF places on her heart. On the most troublesome days, breathing, walking and even talking challenges her.

"My cardiologist is not crazy about me playing sports, but participating in sports has given me a reason to get up in the morning," she said. "Playing sports has basically kept me sane. It has made me healthier mentally and physically. I know my body, and it lets me know when I need to slow down."

During the NWFL 2001 campaign, Sheckells' teammates affectionately nicknamed her "Goose" after her football idol, former Baltimore Ravens defensive tackle Tony Siragusa. She's not only similar to Siragusa in physical stature, she also played defensive the same way he did—extremely tough.

"I enjoy beating up on the center," Sheckells said, with a chuckle. "Football is fun. I love the aggressiveness of the game. When I am on the football field, I feel empowered."

At the end of the 2001 football season, Sheckells and a few of her friends purchased the Burn.

"I bought the team to be a part of the action on a different level," she said. "Football has been hard on my body. I think the 2002 football season will be my last season as a player.* I will then work on developing the team for the next generation of female football players."

In addition to football, Sheckells has participated in several other highly competitive sports. In high school, she received All-County honors in soccer, and All-County and All-Metro in softball. She also played first base for the Baltimore Stars of the Eastern Women's Baseball Conference (EWBC), an amateur hardball league.

If you're looking for a role model for your children, look no further than the courageous Cheryl Sheckells. "Kids don't have to hide from their hardships, they don't have to be ashamed of themselves," she said. "They can get the help they need to overcome any obstacles."

Although Sheckells' life has been fraught with medical problems, it hasn't stopped her from succeeding in sports and inspiring others along the way.

Even though Sheckells stated that she would retire after 2002, she did see limited action during the 2003 and 2004 seasons.

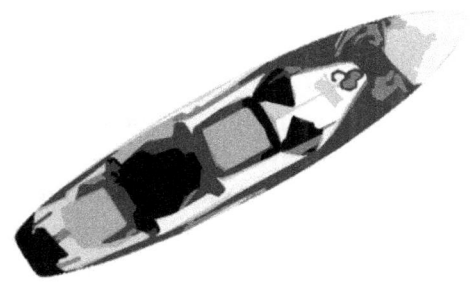

Jesse Billauer

As a youngster growing up in Pacific Palisades, California, Jesse Billauer dominated the playing fields. He excelled in several sports, but surfing was the only one that completely captivated his soul.

Billauer began surfing at approximately nine years old. His brother Josh and friend John Hearne introduced him to the sport. It was love at first ride. Every time he needed an escape from reality, he grabbed his surfboard and headed for the beach. He spent almost all of his free time riding the tranquility of the waves.

At the age of eleven, Billauer began surfing in various competitions along the Southern California Coast. As his abilities increased, so did his success. Surfing sponsorships quickly followed suit. With the help of his supporters, he jumped to the international surfing scene. In the mid nineties, *Surfer Magazine* had branded him one of the top one hundred surfing prospects in the world.

Just as Billauer began to make waves in the surfing world, his career hit an undercurrent in October 1995. While driving to high school one morning, Billauer's Chevy Blazer collided with another car. The violent impact caused his automobile to flip over, propelling him from his vehicle right through the closed driver's side window.

Billauer feared the worst. He thought the accident had paralyzed him. Miraculously, he escaped the wreck with only severe whiplash and a torn ligament in his right thumb. "I was lucky I wasn't seriously injured at that time," Billauer said. "When I got to the hospital, I said, 'please don't let me be paralyzed.'" Ironically, he foreshadowed his own fate without even knowing it.

Billauer recovered from his injuries and returned to competitive surfing. In March of 1996, he earned the number one ranking in the junior division of the Pacific Surf Series.

With a pro tour within reach, Billauer had every reason to feel optimistic. But the dark waves of fate rolled in and triggered an undertow in his future.

On March 25, 1996, Billauer was involved in another accident. This time he wasn't so fortunate. While hanging ten at Zuma Beach, a wave struck him in the back, causing a violent confrontation between his head and neck and an unforgiving sandbar.

Within a split second, Billauer was face down in the water, unable to move or breathe. He held his breath until a wave turned him over, allowing him to breath again and eventually shout for help. He finally got the attention of his friends who pulled him out of the water and stabilized him until medical help arrived.

Billauer suffered a complete C-6 spinal cord injury, leaving him without any sensation or mobility below his mid-chest level, and the minimal use of his upper extremities.

"I didn't know how serious it was," Billauer recalled. "I thought I would be okay after a while. I was scared. After a while, I knew I had to accept what had happened to me."

Even though his future looked bleak, he remained upbeat and positive. He still felt extremely lucky to be alive.

After three months of intense rehabilitation, Billauer returned home. The love and support that he received from his family and friends helped him get through a daunting period in his life.

"I never gave up on myself because I had my friends, family, and the good things in life to help me get through it," he said.

Although it would have been easy to wallow in despair, Billauer refused to let his condition get in the way of living a full and productive existence.

He participated in activities such as ping-pong, hand-cycling, weightlifting, wheelchair tennis, and adaptive surfing to stay active and improve the quality of his life.

In 2002, Billauer earned his bachelors degree in communications from San Diego State University. After college, he ventured into motivational speaking. He now employs his incredible life experiences and presentation skills to captivate and inspire his audiences.

"I got positive feedback from a lot of different people," the charismatic Billauer said. "They told me this (motivational speaking) is something I should do. I'm able to show people that life is a precious thing that shouldn't be taken for granted."

Since his accident, Billauer has created the Life Rolls On Foundation, a nonprofit organization committed to raising funds and awareness for people with spinal cord injuries. Billauer believes that scientific breakthroughs in spinal cord injury research will eventually breed a cure for paralysis.

"I started the Life Rolls On Foundation to raise money for (paralysis) research," the wave warrior said. "I feel one day that people like me will regain some of the use of our paralyzed limbs."

In addition to its educational and philanthropic efforts, Life Rolls On has instituted "They Will Surf Again (TWSA"), an adaptive surfing program for people with spinal cord injuries.

Billauer's amazing resolve is contagious. He reminds us that the only limitations we have are the ones we place on ourselves.

"When I got injured," Billauer said, "I learned a very important lesson; no matter what, life rolls on."

Words to live by, dude!

Andy Parr

I've always been amazed with a skier's ability to race down the slopes under the most treacherous conditions. So when I come across an athlete like Andy Parr, I'm even more impressed.

Parr is a competitive alpine skier. Just like any other ski racer, he navigates difficult and dangerous race courses while traveling at top speeds. There's one factor, though, that makes his job more challenging: he's legally blind.

Parr enjoyed a normal childhood until his vision started to fade at twelve years old. By the time he hit high school, his deteriorating eyesight made learning nearly impossible. He struggled mightily with his studies. No matter how hard he tried, his grades just didn't improve.

He never made the connection between his failing eyesight and poor classroom performance.

"I thought my vision was fine," Parr said. "I figured other people just had better vision than me. It never occurred to me that there might be a real problem with my eyesight."

With the likelihood of college evaporating, Parr decided to enlist in the Marines at the age of eighteen. Unfortunately, his inadequate eyesight caused him to fail the physical, and denied him entry.

A retinal specialist diagnosed him with Stargardt's Disease—a type of macular degeneration that causes a progressive loss of central vision of both eyes, but does not affect peripheral vision.

"I was floored and hurt when I learned of my condition," Parr recounted. "But I eventually picked myself up and got on with my life."

Once Parr realized that a legitimate problem existed with his eyesight, he made the necessary adjustments to learn more efficiently. As a result, his grades improved, enabling him to finish high school.

Parr went on to attend Southern Vermont College, where he made the Dean's list and even spent a semester in his senior year studying at the world-renowned Oxford University in England. In 1995 he graduated from college with a degree in Resort Management and then accepted a job with the well-known Sugarloaf ski resort in Maine.

While working at Sugarloaf, Parr witnessed some of the top downhill skiers in the world compete, including A. J. Kitt, Hillary Lindh, Tommy Moe, and Picabo Street. They inspired him to chase gold with a vengeance.

In the fall of 1999, Parr began training with Chris Devlin-Young, the head coach of the New England Disabled Ski Team. With Devlin-Young's guidance, he captured the New England Championship crown at the 2000 Eastern Regionals in Waterville Valley, New Hampshire.

Two days later at the 2000 Chevy Truck Disabled Alpine Nationals in Mount Snow, Vermont, Parr took home four medals, including the gold for the combined overall. His spectacular performance helped him earn a spot on the 2002 U.S. Disabled Alpine Ski Team.

"When I first made the U.S. team, I did it on pure power and determination," he said. "The coaches helped me polish my craft. I now try to plan my attack. Before a race, I will hit the snow and try to memorize the trail. It gives me the confidence to be aggressive on the slopes."

In 2002 Parr turned his focus to the international racing scene. At the European Cup Races for the Disabled, he won a silver medal and two bronzes.

After a respectable showing on the European racing circuit, Parr competed at the 2002 Paralympics in Salt Lake City, Utah, snatching a silver medal in the Slalom and a bronze in the Giant Slalom.

"I was happy with my performance, but my goal is to win," he said. "I don't want to be second, third, or fourth. I'm out there to win."

At the 2006 Winter Paralympics in Torino, Italy, Parr finished in eighth place in the Men's Giant Slalom for the visually impaired.

While he may not have fulfilled his ultimate aspiration, his valiant performance did help him earn the 2006 U.S. (Male) Paralympic Spirit Award—an honor given to the Paralympian who best represents the Olympic ideals and values during the games. He also served as the head coach for the New England Disabled Ski Team (NEDST) for the 2006-07 season.

Way to go, Andy. Keep pursuing the finish line with extreme valor and velocity in whatever way you choose.

Cody Colchado Jr.

Cody Colchado Jr. was born with a 70-75 percent hearing loss. Fearing ridicule from the other children in school, Colchado refused to wear his hearing aides. As a result, learning was extremely difficult. He eventually learned to read in the seventh grade, due to his mother's devotion and advances in hearing aide technology.

"My early school years were very painful for me," Colchado recollected. "I knew I wasn't dumb. I just needed the proper tools to help me learn. Once I started to wear them (hearing aids), my daily activities became much easier."

An outstanding athlete, Colchado participated in several competitive sports throughout his youth, but enjoyed success as a high school football player.

A devastating injury suffered during a routine football practice in 1981 changed the course of his life. While participating in a tackling drill, Colchado hit his head on a sprinkler, splitting his helmet in two and injuring his head. Soon thereafter, his eyesight began to fade. His doctor told him that the injury would cause a complete loss of vision within eighteen months.

Colchado continued to play center while his eyesight diminished, relying on his teammates to help him lineup against the defense. But his eyesight deteriorated to the point in which his doctor could no longer medically clear him to play football.

Since gridiron action was no longer an option, Colchado turned to the sport of powerlifting to fill a competitive void. At the age of eighteen, he began competing with the United States Association of Blind Athletes (USABA). He powerlifted for four years and then took some time off to recharge his batteries.

After several years away from the sport, Colchado competed at the 1994 World Championships for the Blind in Edmonton, Alberta, Canada, where he captured the World Championship in the 242-pound weight class.

"At my comeback in Edmonton, Canada, not many people knew who I was," he said. "I basically came from out of the blue to win the championship in my weight class. It was such an incredible feeling."

To help him hoist massive amounts of weight, Colchado employs a determined attitude and the collective spirit of visually impaired athletes.

"When I lift, I visualize all blind athletes helping me raise the bar," Colchado said. "Whether the bar is underneath me or on top of me, I feel there's nothing that can stop me from lifting it."

In addition to his powerlifting accomplishments, Colchado has successfully competed in the blind shot-put and blind pentathlon—a five-event athletic competition that tests strength, speed, power, and endurance.

After years of learning difficulties, Colchado is now

pursuing a degree in Adaptive Physical Education from the University of Texas Pan-America, and says he is "enjoying every minute of it." He aspires to help other sensory impaired athletes live out their dreams and live productive lives.

Colchado's resilient spirit is the driving force behind his success. The adversity that he has faced would have daunted the average person. But he's anything but that, possessing a super-human will—an attribute that he claims God gave him.

While the Texas native's behemoth physique is stacked with large, powerful muscles, his strongest attribute beats deep within his chest, helping him raise the bar to its final destination time and again.

Keep pumping to the next level, Cody!

Christine Galan

The majority of the interviews I conduct are done over the phone. So, when I get the opportunity to interview someone in person, I jump at it.

I met with Christine Galan for a hot cup of java in one of New York City's largest coffee establishments.

Although Galan isn't a highly competitive athlete, her athletic achievement is inspiring nonetheless.

Galan's first medical problem surfaced at the age of seventeen, when she developed autoimmune hemolytic anemia—a disorder characterized by the premature destruction of healthy red blood cells. Her condition forced the doctors to remove her spleen and gall bladder.

Then, at twenty-five, lupus—a chronic inflammatory disease that affects various parts of the body—attacked her heart, causing congestive heart failure. Galan's doctor treated her with sizeable amounts of chemotherapy and prednisone to offset the effects of the condition. But, by 1996, her heart and liver deteriorated to the point in which a double transplant became her only option.

On October 23, 1998, after eleven weeks in intensive

care and on the brink of death, Galan received word that a new heart and liver became available for donation.

On October 24, 1998, after a twelve-hour operation, she became the first person in the Western United States to receive a heart and liver transplant.

"I waited and waited and hoped that someone would die so I could live," Galan recalled. "It's such a horrible thing to have to think that way, but my life depended on someone dying. The day I received my organs, I never looked back."

Just eighteen days after she received her new lease on life, Galan miraculously left the hospital and returned home. The following day, she jumped on the treadmill for a light twenty-minute workout and went back to work in her family's advertising specialty business. Soon thereafter, she resumed her daily exercise regimen.

"I contribute my speedy recovery to my healthy lifestyle and my positive thinking," Galan said. "I'm sure if I lived a different lifestyle, I would not be here to tell people my story."

On November 4, 2001, just three years removed from her operation, Galan became the first heart and liver transplant recipient to complete the New York City Marathon. Her extraordinary accomplishment amazed the entire medical community and put her in the media spotlight, as the press provided ample coverage of the event.

"I am not a true runner," Galan said. "I ran the NYC marathon to help raise awareness. I want to inspire people to become organ and tissue donors. I don't want anyone to have to wait for organs for as long as I did."

In addition to her tissue and organ donor advocacy work, Galan volunteers countless hours as wish-granter for the

Starlight Starbright Children's Foundation, where she has helped over two hundred seriously ill children fulfill their dreams. Even when her health started to falter, she still managed to express genuine concern for the children and their wishes.

"I love my work with children," the Jamaican-born Galan said. "It helps me put my life in perspective. When you meet some of these kids, you realize just how challenging their lives really are. Knowing that you have the ability to make them smile makes it worth the effort."

Due to her humble nature, Galan has never seen herself as a role model. With time and encouragement from her peers, she has learned to accept the praise.

"I never thought of myself as a role model until I heard it over and over again," Galan said. "I guess now I can say I am a role model. People have been affected by me in a positive way, and that's what's really important."

On October 24th 1998, Galan received pieces of a stranger and got the opportunity to live a happy, productive life. In return, she continues to give her entire self back to the world.

Mary Bryant

On May 27, 1998, Mary Bryant received a phone call from her friend Diane. She told Bryant that the doctor had diagnosed her with breast cancer.

After Bryant hung up the telephone, she went to the doctor's office to get a suspicious lump on her left breast examined. Noticing a potential problem, the doctor referred her to a breast specialist who immediately sent her for a mammogram and sonogram. That same day, the doctor confirmed her worst fear: The lump was indeed malignant.

"Talk about being bowled over," Bryant recalled. "My doctor just flat out started with 'we have a problem.' I was pretty scared. You know it's (cancer) out there, but you never think it's going to be you."

Two weeks after her diagnosis, doctors performed the necessary surgery to remove the cancer. Although sidelined for six weeks, Bryant eventually made her way back. Utilizing running as her secret weapon against the disease, she refused to let cancer keep her out of the game.

As a testament to her remarkably strong spirit, Bryant

completed her fourth marathon in the midst of six months of intense chemotherapy.

"I was the one that was keeping my body as strong as it could be so that I could fight off this cancer baloney," she said. "My running helped me through it. It was my way of gaining control over my body."

Bryant and Diane made a solemn pact to run the 1999 New York City marathon together. On September 24th, five weeks before the race, Diane succumbed to the dreadful disease. To pay homage to her, Bryant ran the marathon with a wheelchair filled with beautiful pink roses.

"The emotional heaviness of not running the marathon with Diane was hard," Bryant said. "However, I was able to get through it because so many people knew of the story between me and Diane. People ran up to me, hugged me, and thanked me for touching their lives."

Bryant spends countless hours supporting women's health issues and people with disabilities. Perhaps the latter has something to do with her brother Don Supinski, who, at the age of sixteen, was involved in a freak accident, which paralyzed him from the neck down.

In November 1997, with his sister at his side, he became the first man without the use of his arms and legs to enter and complete the NYC marathon. Utilizing an electric wheelchair, Supinski propelled himself the entire distance by pushing his head back into the chair's headrest, activating its motor.

Supinski's courage has motivated Bryant to help people with disabilities take part in running programs. Over the course of her running career, she has participated as a marathon guide for several physically challenged athletes.

"If you can't run, you walk, and if you can't walk, you roll," said Bryant, who is vice president of New York's Achilles Track Club—a worldwide organization that encourages people with various disabilities to compete in mainstream sports. "The point is you use whatever you have to get out there."

On November 6, 2001, at the age of forty-seven, Supinski peacefully passed away.

Throughout her childhood, Bryant dreamed of becoming a glamorous fashion model. Even though her brother's life was fraught with numerous medical challenges, he always found the strength to support his younger sister's aspirations. In fact, she believes that his love and encouragement helped her achieve her goals.

"I was one of those little girls who had a dream to be a model," said Bryant, who has enjoyed a long, successful career as a fashion model with the Ford Agency—one of the top model agencies in the world. "More than anything, I wanted someone to tell me I was pretty. I was hungry for the attention. Every little girl needs attention, but my parents were busy with my brother.

"However, no matter what I did, Don always encouraged me to pursue my dreams. That is one of the reasons why I consider him my hero."

In addition to modeling and her work with the Achilles Track Club, Bryant is a renowned and respected motivational speaker. She draws from her incredible life experiences to help inspire her audiences.

In November 2004 she completed her tenth NYC marathon, and now coaches soldiers who have lost legs in Iraq and Afghanistan for the 26.2 mile trek. Since her initial battle with breast cancer, Bryant's mammograms have all come back negative, which is a credit to her healthy lifestyle, enabling her to cherish life even further.

"What is most important is to stay healthy in eating, exercising and lifestyle, and be sure to keep up with the check-ups," she said. "This June (2008) will be ten years (of remission) for me. What a gift."

Bryant is an inspiration to the young and young at heart. Her incredible positive attitude is infectious. I take my running sneakers off to this amazing woman and radiant road warrior.

Kelly Sutton

If competing in the male-dominated sport of race car driving isn't hard enough, Kelly Sutton does it with the diagnosis of multiple sclerosis (MS)—a potentially debilitating autoimmune disease that attacks the central nervous system (brain and spinal cord) and affects motor skills.

That hasn't stopped Sutton from tearing up the track at speeds up to one hundred and sixty miles per hour.

In 1988, at the age of sixteen, Sutton was diagnosed with relapsing-remitting multiple sclerosis—a form of MS in which the individual experiences episodes of flare-ups (relapses), followed by periods of remission, when symptoms can at least partially disappear or vanish altogether.

Her doctor said that in eight to ten years she would lose the ability to walk. Although concerned, Sutton had her family to help cope with the grim prediction.

"My family and I were devastated by the doctor's prognosis," Sutton recalled. "But we all agreed that we would get through this as a family."

After a three-year hiatus, her father asked if she wanted to pursue a comeback. Sutton told him that she had never lost her love for racing, and was chomping at the bit to return to the track.

From 1992-1994, Sutton won seven feature races, twenty qualifiers, and five pole positions in the Old Dominion Speedway/Pro Mini-Stock Series.

With her racing career heading in the right direction, Sutton had every reason to feel optimistic. But in 1995, she faced another obstacle as a passenger in an automobile accident. The crash triggered an acute MS attack, confining her to a wheelchair for an entire year. She wound up missing approximately a year and half of racing, but eventually returned to the sport stronger and more determined than ever.

"Getting out of that wheelchair and back to racing was probably the greatest accomplishment in my life," she said emphatically.

Sutton's inspirational efforts extend far beyond the track. She spends countless hours educating and motivating people with MS. She also goes out of her way to meet and sign autographs for her loyal fans.

"I feel it's very important for me to give back to the community," the Crownsville, Maryland native said. "I'm very fortunate to be able to pursue my passion even though I have MS. I tell everyone to turn their adversity into something positive."

In 1997 Sutton became the first woman to win a regional or national race in the Allison Legacy Series. Even though she has enjoyed success in a male-dominated sport, she doesn't see herself as female race car driver while chasing the checkered flag.

"Racing is a big part of me, and I want to be looked at

as just another driver, not a female driver," she said. "When I'm out there on the track, I'm simply a driver."

Sutton continues to fight a winning battle against MS. The five-foot-eight driver attributes her good fortune to a healthy lifestyle and an effective drug therapy program. As a result, the mother of two has been able to limit her relapses, allowing her the opportunity to continue her racing career.

In two full seasons (2002-2003) on the NASCAR Goody's Dash Series, Sutton finished in 12th and 8th place, respectively.

In 2004 she shifted gears and entered the NASCAR Craftsman Truck Series (NCTS)—one of the most demanding tours in auto racing. Sutton finished the series in an impressive twenty-sixth place out of a field of one hundred and nine drivers. The following year, she placed twenty-ninth out of ninety-three competitors in the same series, with earnings of $143,949.

In addition to her accomplishments on the track, Sutton has earned several prestigious accolades off the asphalt. In October 2003, the Women's Sports Foundation bestowed her with the Wilma Rudolph Courage Award for her overall inspirational efforts. The following year, Angels Care and the Tempe Sports Authority presented her with the Gene Autry Courage Award—an honor given to extraordinary athletes who have overcome insurmountable odds.

"For a long time, I didn't know why I was handed all this adversity," Sutton said. "But now I know everything happens for a reason. Without some misfortune in my life I would not be the person I am today."

Sutton's amazing resolve and bravery proves she is a winner in the most important race of all: The human race.

Paul Martin

Throughout his youth, Paul Martin had a special knack for finding trouble. His father, an old school disciplinarian, took exception to his son's mischievous behavior and often punished him in ways that Martin felt were totally unnecessary.

While Martin didn't get along with his father, he did share a special bond with his mother. His parents separated, and his mother relocated to another state where she eventually remarried. Her absence put an even greater strain on his relationship with his dad. When he could no longer stand living under his father's iron rule, he moved in with his mother and her new husband.

After a week, the stress of living in cramped quarters forced his mother to ask him to leave.

Martin refused to return to his father and explored the possibility of going into foster care. When Martin was sixteen, a social worker placed him with a friend whose mother was a certified foster parent.

"I was quite the troublemaker in high school," Martin recalled. "I didn't like the way my father disciplined me. I was unhappy living with him and felt being in foster care was my best option at the time. It turned out to be a good experience."

Fortunately for Martin, he had ice hockey—the one aspect of his life that he felt he did well—to help cope with his tumultuous childhood. It provided him with self-confidence and a positive outlet for his adolescent hyperactivity by giving him the opportunity to display his solid goaltending skills.

When Martin was a freshman his high school head coach allowed him to practice with the varsity hockey team and to dress for home games because his puck stopping ability proved him worthy.

But in his junior year, sophomore goalie Troy Hanks, who possessed more talent, joined the team and competed for the starting position. Instead of contending for ice time, Martin quit the Wildcats and began experimenting with drugs.

In his senior year, Martin gradually cleaned up his act and rejoined the Wildcats when Hanks left to join a AAA team. Martin was the best netminder on the squad but was relegated to backup duty because he had missed a year of play and still found time to get into some trouble.

After a few contests, Martin got his opportunity to start. In his first game in net, he blanked the opposition. He added two more shutouts that season and helped his squad make it all the way to the quarterfinals of the Division II Massachusetts State Championship playoffs.

Martin also excelled in the classroom. His impressive SAT score helped him gain entry into the University of Lowell, in Lowell, Massachusetts.

As a freshman, Martin attempted to make the University's

Division I hockey team as a walk-on but fell short. He wound up losing interest in college and eventually dropped out. Martin spent the next two years working as an ironworker before he went back to school to finish his mechanical engineering degree.

After college, Martin secured a well-paying job as a sales engineer for a company that produced welding equipment. While it certainly wasn't his dream occupation, it did provide him with financial stability.

Things were looking up for Martin. Finally, he had some direction. But at twenty-five, his life took an unexpected detour.

One night, after having a few drinks at dinner, Martin fell asleep at the wheel and crashed his car into a fire truck, seriously injuring himself. The accident led to the amputation of his left leg below the knee. After owning up to his mistake and several weeks of deep soul searching, he decided to move on and make the most of his life despite his impairment.

"I chose to apply the attitude of gratitude," he said. "My disability would only be as limiting as I allowed it to be. There are a lot of people who are worse off than me."

Six weeks after his accident, Martin returned to work. Following a period of physical and mental adjustments, he made his way back to the playing field. He started skiing again and even joined an able-bodied ice hockey league in New Jersey.

While able to ski and skate, running still eluded him. Every time Martin took a few strides, his prosthesis loosened. With the help of a specially designed running leg, he was able to jog on a treadmill without that problem.

With a few months of running behind him, Martin decided to challenge himself by entering in his first National Amputee Track and Field Games. And he did well, igniting his desire for further competition. He then entered a sprint triathlon (a shorter triathlon) and finished forty-fourth out of one hundred competitors.

Subsequently, his athletic career reached new heights at the 1995 National Amputee Track and Field Games, where he set a national record in the 1500-meter race with a time of 5:20:88.

Martin developed a passion for distance running, even though the friction between his stump and prosthesis caused him to endure a measure of pain.

Still, he began to train for his next endeavor: The New York City Marathon. On November 12, 1995, he completed the 26.2 trek with a respectable time of 4:47.

Following his gutsy performance, Martin slowly made his way to a park bench and shed exhausted tears of joy. His triumphant New York City day, earned through perspiration and perseverance, helped him realize that he could achieve any realistic goal just as long as he dedicated himself wholeheartedly to it.

After several months of deliberation, Martin decided to quit his job to pursue his passion full-time.

Martin's professional athletic career doesn't include the multi million-dollar contract or the lucrative endorsement deal (although he does have a number of sponsors). And while I'm sure he would love to be a ridiculously high-paid athlete, Martin states that he competes for two simple reasons: He loves sports and the opportunity presents itself.

Nevertheless, Martin has built an impressive athletic

résumé over the years. He is the first amputee athlete to compete on four different national teams: cycling, triathlon, ice hockey, and alpine skiing; he has completed an amazing ten Ironman Triathlons; in 1997, the U.S. Olympic Committee named him the Disabled Athlete of the Year; and at the 2004 Summer Paralympic Games in Athens, Greece, he captured a silver medal in the Men's Cycling Team Sprint and a bronze medal in the Men's 4km Individual Pursuit.

As far as his athletic achievements go, Martin credits his steadfast commitment to sports as the driving force behind his success.

"Heart and will, then athletic prowess got me where I wanted to go," he said. "Put your head where you want the rest of your body to be and it will follow."

Martin and his father have put their differences behind them. He's now one of his son's biggest fans, traveling across the globe to see him compete.

In 2002, Martin penned his successful autobiography: *One Man's Leg*. In 2004, he launched an online coaching company called Amplitude Multisport LLC, which is dedicated to helping clients achieve success in endurance sports.

Martin's accident helped him realize that his happiness comes first and he's in complete control of his destiny; an ideology he highly recommends.

With unmatched bravery, Martin turned on the after burners and spirited to the front of the pack, leaving the rat race in the dust.

Hey, Paul, see you at the finish line.

Afterword

Running Through Roadblocks provided me with the opportunity to interview twenty of the most gracious and inspirational athletes in North America. For this, I'm truly blessed.

When I first began the research for my book, I immediately knew I was in the midst of something special. Each athlete I interviewed helped me find a new appreciation for life. I believe everyone possesses an inner strength that's waiting to be revealed. For some people, it takes a traumatic life-alternating event to awaken the giant within.

I feel these stories needed to be told. I absolutely believe you will gain something valuable from the stories in *Running Through Roadblocks*.

When life constructs a roadblock, lower your head and blast through the barrier that's obstructing your path toward a happy life. You owe it to yourself.

I hope you enjoyed reading *Running Through Roadblocks* as much as I loved writing it. Perhaps, my book will lead to a foundation that exposes children to different sports opportunities.

Thank you for your support!

Jerry Del Priore

Foundations and Businesses

Jesse Billauer
http://www.liferollson.org
400 Corporate Pointe
Suite 300 Los Angeles, CA 90230
866-We Will Walk (866-939-4559)
Fax: 310-943-1918

Jim Eisenreich
http://www.touretts .org
Jim Eisenreich Foundation
PO Box 953
Blue Springs, MO 64013
1 (800) 442-8624

Paul Martin
http://paulmartinspeaks.com/
Phone: 508-720-0648
Fax: 508-653-4964
Paul@paulmartinspeaks.com

Molly McMaster
http://www.Colonclub.com
The Colon Club
17 Peach Tree Lane
Wilton, NY 12831

Grandmaster Paul Mormando
http://www.mormandomartialarts.com

Mormando Martial Arts System
4626 Flatlands Avenue
Brooklyn, NY 11234
718-677-9704
mrkarateusa@aol.com

Sifu Karl Romain
http://www.Romainskungfu.com

Romain's Kung Fu Academy of Nyack
121 Main Street
Nyack, NY 10960
845-353-7800

Mike Utley
http://www.MikeUtley.org

Mike Utley Foundation
Post Office Box 458
Orondo, Washington 98843
Toll Free: 800.294.4683
utley60@aol.com

Sports Terms Glossary

Assist. A player or players (maximum of two) who touched the puck prior to the goal, provided no defender handles or possesses the puck in between, is credit with the point (assist).

Blue Liner. A slang name given to the defensemen that's derived from lining up on the blue line to start a game, playing near the blue line in the offensive zone and protecting the defensive blue line against opposing offensive players.

Blue Lines. The pair of 12-inch wide lines that extend across the ice at a distance of 60 feet from each goal. A blue line sits on either side of the red line, and the area between the two blue lines is the neutral zone.

Cruiserweight/Lightweight. A division for wrestlers who weigh between 185 lbs and 218 lbs. Wrestlers who are less than 185 lbs are in this category as well.

Dinger. Slang terminology for home run.

Gridiron. Slang terminology for football field.

Hat trick. Three goals scored by a single player in one game.

Heel. The professional wrestling personality who plays the role of the villain.

Lit the Lamp. Slang terminology for scoring a goal in hockey.

NASCAR. National Association for Stock Car Auto Racing—the national sanctioning body that governs stock car racing.

Netminder. Slang terminology for goalie in hockey.

Nose Guard. The defensive lineman positioned between the defensive tackles opposite the center on the offensive line.

Paralympics. The Olympics for people with physical disabilities.

Plus/Minus rating. Hockey players earn a plus +1 when they're on the ice when their team scores a goal. They acquire a minus –1 when they're on the ice when their team has a goal scored against them. This is considered the best rating system for a defensive player since they do not score often. Goalies are not included in this system, and a power play goal does not change a player's plus/minus status.

Right Guard. A position on the offensive line in football whose job is to protect the quarterback and block for other offensive players (running backs and receivers).

Round Tripper. Slang terminology for home run.

Sifu. The master instructor in Kung Fu.

The Show. Slang terminology for major league baseball (MLB).

About the Author

Jerry Del Priore is a freelance sports writer from Brooklyn, New York, who covers a variety of professional, college and high school sports for a number of print and online publications.

At the age of twelve, Del Priore developed juvenile diabetes. He now lives an active and healthy lifestyle.

In June of 1991, Del Priore earned his Bachelors of Science degree in Physical Education from Brooklyn College.

Over his professional career, Del Priore has worked with countless special needs children in a variety of recreational settings.

In addition to his professional life, Del Priore volunteers his time reading to children and assisting several prominent charities with fundraising events.

Bedazzled Ink Publishing Company
http://www.bedazzledink.com

Fletching Books
Running Through Roadblocks ○ Jerry Del Priore

Dragonfeather Books
Dragon Drool ○ C.A. Casey
Top of the Key ○ C.A. Casey

coming soon
To Live As Legend ○ Amy M. Smith, Lisa Victoria

www.ingramcontent.com/pod-product-compliance
Lightning Source LLC
Chambersburg PA
CBHW071307040426
42444CB00009B/1904